Life in the World's Biomes

Prairie Plants

by Terri Sievert

Consultant:
Ian A. Ramjohn, PhD
Department of Botany and Microbiology
University of Oklahoma
Norman, Oklahoma

Mankato, Minnesota

Bridgestone Books are published by Capstone Press,
151 Good Counsel Drive, P.O. Box 669, Mankato, Minnesota 56002.
www.capstonepress.com

Library of Congress Cataloging-in-Publication Data
Sievert, Terri.
    Prairie plants / by Terri Sievert.
    p. cm.—(Bridgestone Books. Life in the world's biomes)
    Summary: "Tells about a variety of prairie plants, how they are used, why they are in danger, and
how they are being protected"—Provided by publisher.
    Includes bibliographical references and index.
    ISBN 0-7368-4323-X (hardcover)
    1. Prairie plants—Juvenile literature. 2. Prairie plants—North America—Juvenile literature. I. Title.
II. Series: Life in the world's biomes.
QK938.P7S554 2006
581.7'44—dc22   2004029137

Editorial Credits
Amber Bannerman, editor; Jennifer Bergstrom, designer; Kelly Garvin, photo researcher;
    Scott Thoms, photo editor

Photo Credits
Brand X Pictures/David Lorenz Winston, 1
Corbis/Hal Horwitz, 6 (left)
Dwight R. Kuhn, 12
Gilbert S. Grant, 6 (top right)
Image Ideas Inc., 14
James P. Rowan, 4, 6 (bottom right), 8
Lynn M. Stone, 20
Minden Pictures/Jim Brandenburg, cover
OneBlueShoe, 18
Photodisc, 16
Tom & Pat Leeson, 10

1 2 3 4 5 6 10 09 08 07 06 05

Table of Contents

4

Prairies

Tall grass sways in the wind. Grasses and flowers root firmly in the prairie's rich soil. Few trees dot the land. **Pioneers** who first saw the prairie called it a "sea of grass."

The North American prairie stretches from Saskatchewan, Canada, to Texas in the United States. The tall-grass prairie is in the east. The short-grass prairie lies to the west. Between them is a mixed prairie of both tall and short grasses. The mixed-grass prairie is also in southern Saskatchewan and Manitoba, Canada.

◄ Grass gently sways on a North Dakota prairie.

Prairie Plants

Grasses are the most common plants in prairies. Tall-grass plants grow in damp areas. Big bluestem grass can grow more than 10 feet (3 meters) tall. Grasses are shorter on prairies that get less rain. Grama grass grows less than 1 foot (0.3 meter) tall. It is found on short-grass and mixed-grass prairies.

Other plants grow on prairies too. Milkweed and spiderwort plants are common in tall-grass prairies. Blazing star flowers and prairie smoke flowers add color to the land.

◄ Purple spiderworts (left), blue grama grass (top right), and big bluestem grass (bottom right) grow on prairies.

Prairie Plant Features

Leaves and stems help prairie plants stay alive. The yellow coneflower's leaves are narrow. The thin leaves do not dry out in the hot summer sun. The coneflower's stem has tiny hairs on it. The plant stays cool because sunlight bounces off the hairs.

Prairie plants have deep roots. The deep roots of big bluestem grass help it reach water when little rain falls. Deep roots also help the plant live during prairie fires. The top of the plant burns, but the roots do not. After a fire, new plants grow from the roots.

◄ The yellow coneflower can grow up to 5 feet (1.5 meters) tall.

Homes for Animals

Prairie dogs live among some plant roots. They dig tunnels that help these plants live. When rain falls, water runs through the tunnels. The tunnels help rainwater reach deep plant roots.

Other animals make homes in prairie grasses. Birds such as killdeer build small nests in prairie grass. Antelope also make beds there.

◀ Prairie dogs come out of their tunnels during the day to eat.

Plants as Food

Prairie plant stems, flowers, and seeds are food for animals. Antelope eat young, tender shoots of grass. Buffalo **graze** on buffalo grass. Prairie dogs eat grass, flowers, and seeds. Bees gather **pollen** from flowers, such as blazing stars. Aster flowers provide **nectar** for butterflies.

Monarch butterflies lay eggs on milkweed plants. Caterpillars come out of the eggs when they **hatch**. Caterpillars then eat the milkweed plant leaves.

◄ Milkweed plant leaves are the only food a monarch caterpillar will eat.

Plants Used by People

Some prairie plants are commonly used today. Echinacea, also known as the purple coneflower, is used to treat colds. Peppermint oil is made from the mint plant. This oil is used to treat rashes and sunburns.

Native Americans and pioneers used prairie plants for food. They ate wild turnip and nodding wild onion. They made sugar from milkweed flowers.

◀ Native Americans first used echinacea for snakebites and sore throats.

Plants in Danger

Prairies and prairie plants are in danger. Many prairies have been made into farmland. Some plants, like the prairie bush clover, are now **threatened**. Plants like the bush clover can be used to study medicines. Without prairie bush clovers, researchers might not be able to find new medicines.

◄ Farmers plant and harvest crops on land where prairie plants used to grow.

KASOTA PRAIRIE
STATE NATURAL AREA

MINNESOTA DEPARTMENT
OF NATURAL RESOURCES

Protecting Prairie Plants

Canada and the United States protect some of the remaining prairie land. This land cannot be used for farming or building. Prairie bush clovers grow in prairie **preserves**. Park rangers carefully burn and take care of preserves to help prairie plants grow.

Some prairie plants are being saved in smaller areas. Fields of prairie plants grow at nature centers. Children plant prairie grasses and wildflowers next to schools. Many people help save the "sea of grass."

◄ Some prairies are protected by the state. People who harm protected areas are fined.

The Amazing Compass Plant

The tall compass plant helped pioneers find their way on the prairie. Large leaves grow on either side of its long stem. The leaves on one side of the compass plant point north. The leaves on the other side point south. This plant's leaves helped people find which direction they needed to go.

◀ The compass plant has spiky large green leaves. This compass plant grows among wildflowers.

Glossary

graze (GRAYZ)—to eat grass and other plants

hatch (HACH)—to break out of an egg

nectar (NEK-tur)—a sweet liquid in flowers

pioneer (pye-o-NEER)—a person who is among the first to settle a new land

pollen (POL-uhn)—tiny grains that flowers produce

preserve (pri-ZURV)—an area of land set aside by the government for a special purpose, such as protecting plants and animals

threatened (THRET-uhnd)—in danger of dying out

Read More

Hoare, Ben. *Temperate Grasslands.* Biomes Atlases. Austin, Texas: Raintree Steck-Vaughn, 2003.

Mader, Jan. *Living on a Prairie.* Rookie Read-About Geography. New York: Children's Press, 2004.

Internet Sites

FactHound offers a safe, fun way to find Internet sites related to this book. All of the sites on FactHound have been researched by our staff.

Here's how:
1. Visit *www.facthound.com*
2. Type in this special code **073684323X** for age-appropriate sites. Or enter a search word related to this book for a more general search.
3. Click on the **Fetch It** button.

FactHound will fetch the best sites for you!

Index